Leadership Ninja for Teens
A Ninja Life Hacks Guide to Unlocking the Leader Within

Dedicated to every teen who's ever doubted they could lead, you already are. Keep showing up, growing, and leading with heart.

Also by Mary Nhin:

Resilient Ninja | Business Ninja | Emotions Ninja for Teens | Growth Mindset Ninja for Teens | Leadership Ninja for Teens | Self-Management Ninja for Teens | Self-Awareness Ninja for Teens | Social Awareness Ninja for Teens | Decision-MakingNinja for Teens | Relationship Ninja for Teens | Money Ninja for Teens | Angry Ninja | Inventor Ninja | Positive Ninja | Lazy Ninja | Helpful Ninja | Grumpy Ninja | Earth Ninja | Kind Ninja | Perfect Ninja | Anxious Ninja | Money Ninja | Gritty Ninja | Dishonest Ninja | Shy Ninja | Unplugged Ninja | Diversity Ninja | Inclusive Ninja | Masked Ninja | Grateful Ninja | Hangry Ninja | Focused Ninja | Calm Ninja | Brave Ninja | Worry Ninja | Funny Ninja | Patient Ninja | Organized Ninja | Communication Ninja | Stressed Ninja | Smart Ninja | Hopeful Ninja | Confident Ninja | Zen Ninja | Goal-setting | Lonely Ninja | Self-Disciplined Ninja | Motivated Ninja | Sad Ninja | Impulsive Ninja | Feelings Ninja | Creative Ninja | Forgetful Ninja | Nervous Ninja | Emotionally Intelligent Ninja | Growth Mindset Ninja | Jealous Ninja | Frustrated Ninja | Memory Ninja | Listening Ninja | Innovative Ninja | Supportive Ninja | Love Ninja | Humble Ninja | Quiet Ninja | Compassionate Ninja | Sharing Ninja | Caring Ninja | Curious Ninja | Hard-working Ninja | Investments | Problem-Solving Ninja | Integrity Ninja | Disappointed Ninja | eNinja | Healthy Ninja | Adaptable Ninja | Respectful Ninja | Flexible Thinking Ninja | Entrepreneur Ninja | Accountable Ninja | Consent Ninja | Negative Ninja | Sensory Ninja | Tired Ninja | Social Ninja | Neurodivergent Ninja | Happy Ninja | Visionary Ninja | Passionate Ninja | Honest Ninja | Authentic Ninja | Loyal Ninja | Debate Ninja | Collaborative Ninja | Distracted Ninja | Embarrassed Ninja | Negotiator Ninja | Cooperative Ninja | Furious Ninja | Scared Ninja | I Love You, Little Ninja | Gritty Ninja and the St. Patrick's Day Race | Kind Ninja and the Easter Egg Hunt | I Love You, Mom - Earth Ninja | I Love You, Dad - Grumpy Ninja | Patient Ninja's Halloween | Grateful Ninja's Thanksgiving | Ninja Life Hacks Christmas | Ninjas Know the CBT Triangle | Ninjas Go to the Dentist | Ninjas Go to Europe | Ninja Go Camping | Ninjas Go to the Library | Ninjas Go Through a Ninja Warrior Obstacle Course | Ninjas Go to a Party | Ninjas Go to Space | Ninjas Go to Work | Ninjas Go to School | Ninja Life Hacks Numbers | Ninja Life Hacks ABCs of Feelings | Ninja Life Hacks Shapes | Ninja Life Hacks Colors | Ninja Life Hacks Body Parts | Ninja Life Hacks Animals | Ninja Life Hacks Opposites | Ninja Life Hacks Weather | Unplugged Ninja in Vietnam |Kind Ninja Builds a Buddy Bench | Magical Mistake Machine | Lunar New Year | Happy Birthday Ninja | Ninja's New Year | Chef Ninja | Engineer Ninja | Teacher Ninja | Doctor Ninja | Firefighter Ninja | Police Officer Ninja | President Ninja | Coding Ninja | Neurologist Ninja | Amelia Earhart | Steve Jobs | Elon Musk | Indra Nooyi | Anne Frank | Serena Williams | Albert Einstein | Mae Jemison | Frida Kahlo | Michael Jordan | Jane Goodall | Helen Keller | Muhammad Ali | The Wright Brothers | Kobe Bryant | Rosa Parks | Ray Kroc | Martin Luther King, Jr. | Michelle Obama | Sara Blakely | Barack Obama | Walt Disney | Peggy Cherng | David Bowie | Mia Hamm | Sam Walton | Tiger Woods | Jackie Robinson | Mother Teresa | Harriet Tubman | Chloe Kim | Neil Armstrong | Ella Fitzgerald | Stevie Wonder | Maya Angelou | Wilma Rudolph | Lionel Messi | Cristiano Ronaldo | Sophie Cruz | Taylor Swift | Sonia Gandhi | Never Ever Marry a Mermaid | Never Ever Lick a Llama | Never Ever Upset a Unicorn | Never Ever Massage a Moose | Never Ever Dance with Dracula | Never Ever Tickle a Turkey | Never Ever Race a Reindeer

Leadership Ninja for Teens
A Ninja Life Hacks Guide to Unlocking the Leader Within

by Mary Nhin

Leadership Ninja for Teens: A Ninja Life Hacks Guide to Unlocking the Leader Within
© 2025 Mary Nhin | Ninja Life Hacks
All rights reserved.

No part of this book may be reproduced, distributed, or transmitted in any form or by any means, including photocopying, recording, or other electronic or mechanical methods, without the prior written permission of the publisher, except in the case of brief quotations embodied in critical reviews and certain other noncommercial uses permitted by copyright law.

For permission requests, please contact the publisher at:
Grow Grit Press LLC
info@ninjalifehacks.tv

First Edition: 2025
Paperback ISBN: 979-8-89614-136-5
Hardcover ISBN: 979-8-89614-138-9
eBook ISBN: 979-8-89614-137-2

Published by:
Grow Grit Press LLC

ninjalifehacks.tv

Disclaimer: The information provided in this book is based on the author's personal experiences and research. It is intended for educational and informational purposes only. The author and publisher make no guarantees of success or improvement from applying the strategies outlined in this book. Readers are encouraged to consult professionals before making health, financial, legal, or business decisions. Some stories in this book are inspired by real events or composite experiences from friends, students, etc. They're meant to illustrate typical teen challenges.

Printed in the United States of America.

TABLE OF CONTENTS

Author's Note	9
Introduction	11
Part I: Building the Leader Within	13
Chapter 1: Focus – Stay in the Zone	15
Chapter 2: Courage – Courage Over Comfort	25
Chapter 3: Integrity – Leading With Truth	35
Chapter 4: Organization– Structure is Power	43
Chapter 5: Effort – Effort Over Intelligence	53
Chapter 6: Calm – Breathe. Stretch. Reset.	65
Part II: Impacting Others With Your Leadership	75
Chapter 7: Collaboration – The Power of T.E.A.M.	77
Chapter 8: Gratitude – The Magic of Appreciation	87
Chapter 9: Communication – Use the C.L.U.E.	97
Final Thoughts	107
Leadership Ninja Glossary	108
Leadership Ninja Challenges	110
About the Author	113

AUTHOR'S NOTE

Dear Reader,

Writing this book was a journey that took me back to my own teenage years, the challenges, the insecurities, the wins, and the "oops" moments. It reminded me that leadership isn't something you magically gain overnight. It's built moment by moment, choice by choice.

    I created the Ninja Life Hacks series to help kids and teens like you navigate real-life emotions, habits, and situations with confidence and heart. *Leadership Ninja for Teens* is special to me because it combines everything I've learned as an author, entrepreneur, parent, and lifelong student of personal growth.

    My hope is that this book helped you discover your inner leader, the part of you that is capable, kind, brave, focused, and growing stronger every day. Even when life gets messy or hard, you always have tools in your Ninja toolbox.

    Thank you for reading. Thank you for showing up. And thank you for being the kind of leader this world truly needs.

With gratitude, Mary Nhin

INTRODUCTION

Let's be real, leadership might sound like something only adults, CEOs, or class presidents worry about. But here's the secret: Leadership isn't about titles or being the loudest in the room. It's about how you live, how you treat people, and how you show up for yourself.

You're already leading in small ways. When you stay calm during a disagreement, organize your day, or bounce back from a mistake, you're practicing leadership. This book is your guide to making those moments stronger, smarter, and more intentional.

In *Leadership Ninja for Teens*, you'll meet nine different Ninja personalities who each represent a skill or mindset you need to lead your life with confidence. From handling hangry moods to building courage, from focusing your energy to staying calm under pressure, each chapter gives you tools, stories, and strategies you can use right away.

Whether you're navigating school stress, sports pressure, friend drama, or your future dreams, this book is here to help you:

- Take control of your mindset
- Build better habits
- Strengthen your relationships
- Step into the leader you're meant to be

Let's build your Ninja toolbox. Let's lead your life. Let's go, Leadership Ninja.

PART I

BUILDING THE LEADER WITHIN

1

FOCUS

The Power of Focus

In a world filled with pings, posts, and pop-ups, staying focused is a superpower. Focus is the gatekeeper of greatness. Without it, even the most talented minds drift. With it, ordinary students become extraordinary creators. Focus helps you *stay in the game* when your mind wants to check out. Focus helps you finish what you start, show up as your best self, and feel less stressed. Whether you're studying, practicing a skill, or having a conversation, focus is how you stay present, and get results.

Teens who can focus develop stronger habits, get better grades, and feel more in control of their time. Focus doesn't mean perfection, it just means giving your full attention to one thing at a time. That's where the magic happens.

Focus also helps you enter what's known as **the zone** or a **flow state**, a mental state where everything else fades away, and you're completely absorbed in what you're doing. Time flies. Distractions disappear. You're fully in the moment, doing your best work without even thinking about it. This is where confidence builds and big progress happens.

When you train your brain to focus, it becomes easier to get into this zone more often. That's when school feels smoother, your sport becomes more enjoyable, and your creative projects take off. Teens who know how to focus can reduce stress, increase productivity, and get more satisfaction from their efforts.

Why Focus Is a Leadership Superpower

Being a leader means juggling a lot, school, activities, friends, responsibilities, and goals. With so much going on, focus isn't just helpful, it's essential. Focus is what helps leaders cut through the noise, make smart decisions, and actually get things done.

When you're focused, you're not just reacting to what's around you. You're *choosing* where to put your attention. That means you can finish a project, lead a team, or support a friend without getting pulled in a million different directions. In other words, focus helps you show up fully.

Leaders also deal with pressure. Whether it's speaking in front of a group, planning an event, or solving a problem, being able to tune out distractions and stay calm under stress is a huge advantage. Focus helps you stay grounded so you can think clearly, even when things don't go as planned.

And here's the cool part: when you focus, you can get into something called *flow*, a state where you're so locked in that time flies, ideas come faster, and everything just *clicks*. Great athletes, artists, writers, and yes, leaders, all know the power of getting in the zone.

But focus isn't just about performance. It's also about presence. Being a focused leader means listening when someone's talking. It means noticing who's left out, seeing what needs to be done, and caring enough to act. It's how you lead with both your mind and your heart.

So if you want to stand out as a leader, not just be busy, but be *effective*, building your focus muscle is key. And the good news? Focus can be trained. One decision, one breath, one moment at a time.

If Focus Is So Important... Why Is It So Hard?

Let's be real, most teens *know* they should focus. Teachers talk about it, parents nag about it, and every productivity video says the same thing: focus is key. So why aren't more teens actually doing it?

First off, the world is loud. Social media, texts, YouTube, games, ads, group chats, your brain is basically living inside a pinball machine. Every notification pulls your attention away from what you're trying to do, and by the time you get back, you've lost momentum. It's not that you don't *want* to focus, it's that you're being pulled in a dozen directions every second.

Another reason? Focusing feels uncomfortable at first. It takes mental energy to block out distractions and stick with something hard or boring. Sometimes your brain craves quick rewards, like scrolling or snacking, instead of pushing through a tricky math problem or finishing that essay. It's totally normal, but it's also trainable.

And honestly, not a lot of teens are taught *how* to focus. People might say "stop being distracted," but that's like telling someone to swim without teaching them how to float. Focus is a skill, not a personality trait. You can build it with practice, strategies, and patience, just like you'd train for a sport or learn an instrument.

Also, stress, hunger, lack of sleep, and emotions can all mess with your focus. If you're overwhelmed, tired, or dealing with something heavy, it's going to be harder to concentrate. Taking care of your body and emotions makes focusing way easier.

Here's the good news: if focus is hard for you, that doesn't mean you're lazy or bad at school. It means you're human, and you've got room to grow. Every time you practice choosing what to pay attention to, you're strengthening your focus muscle. And that's how leaders are built.

The Sneaky Consequences of Distraction

Distraction is one of the biggest silent blockers to leadership. It doesn't always crash into your day with alarms blaring, it sneaks in quietly. One second you're doing homework, the next you're watching a two-minute video that somehow turns into a 45-minute scroll through your feed. It happens to everyone, but here's the catch: every distraction takes a toll.

Multitasking might feel like a superpower, listening to music, checking texts, working on an essay, but studies show it actually slows you down and leads to more mistakes. Your brain isn't switching between tasks, it's stopping and starting over and over again. That wastes mental energy and drains your focus faster than you realize.

When distractions take over, your momentum disappears. You start things and don't finish them. You feel busy but not productive. Over time, this adds up to something bigger: stress. Unfinished tasks pile up. Your brain starts to feel scrambled. And you may even begin doubting your ability to stay on top of things at all.

Leaders can't afford to live in distraction mode. If you're constantly pulled in a million directions, you can't bring your full energy to what matters most. Focus is how you build progress, and progress builds confidence. When you learn to recognize distractions and gently steer your brain back to the task at hand, you train yourself to be intentional, calm, and in control.

You don't need to be perfect, you just need to be aware. Even small changes, like turning off notifications or setting timers for focused work, can have a big impact. Leaders don't just react, they choose where their attention goes.

Expert Advice

"The teenage brain is still developing its ability to manage attention. But the more you train it, just like a muscle, the better your focus becomes." — Dr. Daniel Siegel, clinical professor of psychiatry and brain development

Actionable Strategies

F.O.C.U.S.
Develop your focus muscle with this ninja life hack.

F: Find distractions and eliminate them. Turn off notifications. Move your phone. Close extra tabs. Silence the noise so your brain can focus.

O: Organize. Create a to-do list, set a timer, or use a planner. Clarity = power.

C: Choose leafy vegetables and healthy foods. Leafy greens, nuts, and berries fuel your brain better than chips and soda.

U: Use exercise to give your brain a boost. A quick walk, stretch, or dance break improves memory and focus.

S: Split up large assignments into smaller tasks. Small wins help you stay motivated. One step at a time adds up fast.

Relatable Teen Scenarios

- Dante started homework with YouTube in the background. Two hours later, he had one paragraph written and didn't remember what he watched.
- Amina set a 25-minute timer to work on her essay, followed by a 5-minute break. In two hours, she finished it and had time to relax.

"The successful warrior is the average person with laser-like focus." — Bruce Lee

Personal Story: My First Book and the Focus Breakthrough

When I started writing my first book, I was *pumped*. I had all these ideas buzzing around in my head, a cool title, and a message I couldn't wait to share. But once I actually sat down to write, the excitement fizzled. I'd stare at the blank screen, then get distracted, by my phone, a snack, or suddenly remembering I "had" to clean my room. I'd write a few pages, then quit halfway through. Days passed. Then weeks. I told myself I was "too busy," but deep down, I was just stuck.

Eventually, I realized I was trying to tackle the whole mountain at once instead of taking it step by step. So I tried something different. I broke the book-writing process down into small, bite-sized pieces. I created a checklist with tasks like "Outline Chapter 1," "Write 300 words today," or "Edit one page." And I promised myself I'd just focus on *one box at a time*, not the whole project.

Every time I checked something off, I felt this little spark of accomplishment. That spark kept me going. It built momentum. The more I *focused on just the next step*, the less overwhelmed I felt. I wasn't pushing myself harder, I was working *smarter*.

That's when it really hit me: focus doesn't mean locking yourself in a room and grinding non-stop. It means choosing where your energy goes and protecting that choice. For me, focus turned a half-finished idea into a published book. And now, whenever I feel overwhelmed, I remember, big things happen one focused step at a time.

Quick Quiz Box

True or False

1. Multitasking improves focus.
2. Exercise can help your brain concentrate.
3. Splitting tasks into chunks can increase motivation.

(Answers: F, T, T)

Journal Reflection Box

What distracts you the most when trying to focus? What's one step you can take to eliminate it?

Action Challenge Chart

Task	Goal	Outcome
Turn off all phone notifications	Remove distractions	Stayed focused for longer
Eat a healthy lunch	Fuel your brain	Felt more clear-headed
Break homework into small steps	Make progress feel doable	Finished earlier and felt proud

Mini-FAQ

Q1: What if I have ADHD or struggle to focus?
A: Start small. Use visual tools, timers, and breaks. Focus is a skill you can build over time.

Q2: How long should I try to focus at once?
A: Try the 25-5 method: 25 minutes of work, 5-minute break. Repeat.

Q3: Can food really affect focus?
A: Absolutely. Healthy fats, protein, and greens support brain power.

Leadership Ninja Takeaway

Brains get better with effort. Keep showing up, and you'll surprise yourself.

2

COURAGE

Courage Over Comfort

Everyone feels fear. But bravery is what you do in the face of fear. It's standing up when it's easier to sit down. It's trying again after failing. It's being yourself when the world pressures you to blend in.

Courage helps you lead others, speak your truth, and chase your goals, even when you're nervous. And the best part? Courage is like a muscle, the more you use it, the stronger it grows.

Why Courage Is a Game-Changer for Leaders

Leadership isn't about being the loudest person in the room or having all the answers, it's about doing what's right, even when it's hard. And that takes courage.

Courage is what helps leaders speak up when no one else will. It's raising your hand with a new idea, even if you're not sure it's perfect. It's standing up for someone being treated unfairly, even if your voice shakes. Without courage, leaders stay silent, play it safe, and miss the chance to make a difference.

Courage also helps you grow. Every time you try something new, take a risk, or face a fear, you're stretching your comfort zone. And that's where growth lives. Whether you're auditioning for a play, running for student council, or just having a tough conversation with a friend, courage helps you move forward.

Plus, courage is contagious. When people see a leader being brave, it inspires them to be brave too. Your courage can spark action in others, create change, and build trust. That's powerful.

But here's the thing: being brave doesn't mean you're fearless. It means you *feel* the fear, and do it anyway. It means choosing purpose over comfort and values over popularity. That's the kind of leadership that lasts.

So whether you're facing failure, uncertainty, or just your own self-doubt, courage helps you step up and lead with heart. And the more you practice it, the stronger it gets.

If Courage Is So Important… Why Is It So Hard?

Let's be honest: being brave sounds awesome. Standing up for yourself, taking big risks, chasing your dreams, it's what all the movies and motivational posters talk about. But when you're actually in the moment? Courage feels scary. And that's exactly why it's tough for a lot of teens.

One big reason is fear of judgment. Most teens care what others think (even if they don't say it out loud). It's normal. But that fear can be powerful enough to stop someone from speaking up in class, sharing an opinion, or even being themselves. The risk of being laughed at or misunderstood often feels way bigger than the reward of being brave.

Another reason is fear of failure. Courage usually involves doing something you're not 100% sure you'll succeed at, trying out for the team, applying for a position, admitting a mistake. And let's be real, no one enjoys failing. But the truth is, failing isn't the opposite of success. It's *part* of success. Still, that's a lesson many teens are just starting to learn.

Also, a lot of people think courage means doing something huge and dramatic. But most courage is quiet and personal. It's apologizing when you're wrong. It's asking for help. It's standing up for someone who's left out. These moments matter just as much, but they're easy to overlook or avoid.

Finally, many teens just don't realize how courageous they already are. Navigating school, friendships, family, social media, and personal challenges every day *takes courage*. But because bravery doesn't always come with a spotlight, it often goes unnoticed, even by the person living it.

The good news? Courage is a muscle. The more you use it in small ways, the stronger it gets. Every time you step out of your comfort zone, you're becoming more confident, more powerful, and more ready to lead.

The Sneaky Consequences of Avoiding Courage

It's totally normal to feel nervous about doing something brave, raising your hand in class, standing up for someone, trying out for the team, or admitting you made a mistake. But when avoiding fear becomes a habit, it slowly chips away at your potential. Every time you say "never mind" or "I'll just stay quiet," you may feel safer in the moment, but long term, you're building a cage made of self-doubt.

Avoiding courage shrinks your confidence. It teaches your brain that fear is something to obey instead of overcome. The more you dodge uncomfortable moments, the scarier they start to feel. Eventually, even small risks can seem huge because you've trained yourself to back away from them.

Over time, this leads to bigger consequences. You might start doubting yourself even in situations where you used to feel confident. Opportunities pass you by, not because you're not capable, but because you've stopped believing you are. And that "what if" feeling? It lingers. You wonder what would've happened if you'd spoken up, taken the shot, or gone for it.

Leaders aren't fearless, they just learn to do things scared. They know courage isn't about being 100% sure. It's about being willing to act even when you're nervous, shaky, or unsure of the outcome. And every time you act with courage, no matter how small, you take back a little power from fear.

The sneaky truth is: avoiding courage doesn't keep you safe, it keeps you stuck. Bravery is like a muscle. Use it, and it grows. Avoid it, and it fades. And you? You were meant to grow.

Expert Advice

"Courage doesn't mean you're not afraid, it means you act anyway. When teens learn to manage fear with their body and breath, they unlock confidence from the inside out." — Dr. Susan David, psychologist and author of *Emotional Agility*

Actionable Strategies

The **B.R.A.V.E. Method**
Practice courage with these five quick steps.

B: Breathe
Take 3 slow breaths to calm your nervous system.

R: Relax your muscles
Drop your shoulders. Unclench your jaw. Wiggle your toes.

A: Adopt positive body language
Stand tall. Chin up. Roll your shoulders back. Your posture affects your confidence.

V: Visualize your success
Picture yourself doing the brave thing, and succeeding.

E: Embrace a mantra
Repeat a phrase like "I can do this," or "Brave means showing up."

Relatable Teen Scenarios

- Eli was nervous to try out for the debate team. He used B.R.A.V.E. before walking on stage, and nailed it.
- Taylor wanted to tell her friend she was upset, but it felt scary. She visualized the convo going well, took a deep breath, and spoke up.

"**Courage** doesn't always roar. Sometimes courage is the quiet voice at the end of the day saying, 'I will try again tomorrow.'" — Mary Anne Radmacher

Personal Story: My First Speech

The first time I gave a speech in front of a crowd, I honestly thought my knees were going to buckle. I could feel every heartbeat like a drum in my chest. My palms were sweaty, my voice trembled, and halfway through my first sentence, I blanked. Totally froze. My mind went silent even though I had practiced that speech dozens of times.

For a split second, I wanted to run. My inner critic was screaming: "You're blowing it!" But then I remembered the one thing I told myself before stepping on stage: *Just show up*. Not "be perfect." Not "impress everyone." Just… show up.

So I took a deep breath. I smiled, even though I was shaking inside. I scanned the room, found a few friendly faces, and started again. I stumbled a little, but I kept going. I made it to the end. And when I finished, the applause wasn't huge, but it was real.

That speech wasn't flawless. I forgot a line, rushed some parts, and definitely didn't win any awards. But I did something way more important: I didn't give up. I showed up scared. I finished anyway. And that changed everything.

After that, I realized something powerful, being brave doesn't mean not being scared. It means feeling the fear and doing it anyway. That experience didn't erase my nerves overnight, but it planted a seed. Each time I faced something scary after that, whether it was a tough conversation, a new challenge, or another speech, I was just a little braver. Not because I nailed it, but because I *tried*.

That first speech wasn't just about public speaking. It was my first real investment in courage, and the returns? They've kept growing ever since.

Quick Quiz Box

True or False

1. Being brave means never feeling afraid.
2. Positive body language can boost confidence.
3. Visualizing success is a waste of time.

(Answers: F, T, F)

Journal Reflection Box

What's one small, brave thing you want to do this week? What's holding you back?

Action Challenge Chart

Task	Goal	Outcome
Use the B.R.A.V.E. method	Face a fear	Felt empowered and calm
Try something out of comfort zone	Build courage muscle	Gained new confidence
Speak up or stand up	Show leadership	Felt proud for being authentic

Mini-FAQ

Q1: What if I try and fail?
A: That's still brave. Courage is about effort, not perfection.

Q2: What if my heart races or I freeze?
A: That's normal! Use B.R.A.V.E. to calm your body and keep going.

Q3: Can bravery be quiet?
A: Absolutely. Sometimes bravery is asking for help or saying, "I need a break."

Leadership Ninja Takeaway

You're braver than you think.
Show up scared, and do it anyway.

COURAGE

3

INTEGRITY

Leading With Truth

Integrity is doing the right thing, even when no one is watching. It's choosing honesty over shortcuts, values over popularity, and character over convenience. Leaders with integrity earn trust, and trust is the foundation of all great leadership.

Integrity helps you sleep at night. It gives you the confidence to stand by your decisions because you know they came from a place of truth. It also makes your voice matter more. When people know you're honest and dependable, they're more likely to follow you, listen to you, and respect you.

A leader without integrity is like a building with no foundation. Things may look fine on the outside, but the moment pressure hits, everything falls apart. Leaders make tough decisions. They face temptations. And they often influence others. Without integrity, that influence can lead to broken trust, damaged relationships, and a reputation that's hard to fix.

Integrity also creates consistency. When your actions match your values, people know what to expect. That predictability builds security in teams and relationships. Integrity gives your leadership power that doesn't fade, even when you make mistakes.

If Integrity Is So Important... Why Is It So Hard?

Integrity isn't always easy. Sometimes telling the truth feels risky. Sometimes it's tempting to take a shortcut to win or avoid getting in trouble. In school, sports, or friendships, you might feel pressure to blend in, cover up a mistake, or go along with the crowd. And let's be real: integrity doesn't always come with instant rewards. In fact, sometimes it can make things harder in the moment.

That's why integrity takes courage. It's choosing to be real in a world that sometimes celebrates fake. It's choosing long-term respect over short-term approval. But every time you make that choice, your character gets stronger, your leadership grows, and you become someone others can truly count on.

The Sneaky Consequences of Cutting Corners

When you break trust, even in small ways, people notice. Maybe you "borrow" answers on a quiz or say what someone wants to hear instead of the truth. At first, it seems harmless. But each time you cut a corner, you chip away at your character. And when bigger decisions come, you may not have the habit or the courage to choose what's right.

Cutting corners can:

» Damage your reputation
» Lead to more stress from trying to keep up lies or excuses
» Make people doubt your word or intentions
» Lead to guilt or anxiety from living out of alignment with your values
» Integrity isn't about being perfect. It's about being honest, even when it's uncomfortable.

Expert Advice

"Integrity is doing the right thing, even when it's hard. It builds real confidence because you're not pretending to be someone you're not." — Dr. Brené Brown, research professor and author

Actionable Strategy

Keep promises and be honest, that's integrity.

Integrity isn't complicated, it's about doing the right thing, even when no one is watching. That starts with two simple but powerful actions:

- » **Keep your promises.** If you say you'll do something, do it. Following through builds trust and shows people they can count on you. If something changes, don't disappear, communicate and take responsibility.
- » **Be honest.** Tell the truth, even when it's hard. Own your mistakes instead of hiding them. Being real builds respect and shows that you value truth over pretending.

These two habits, keeping your word and telling the truth, are the foundation of integrity. They help you earn trust, lead by example, and become someone others admire and want to follow.

Relatable Teen Scenario

Jordan saw their best friend cheating on a test and didn't know what to do. They didn't want to be a snitch, but they also felt sick inside knowing it wasn't right. Later, Jordan talked privately with their friend, saying, "I care about you, but this doesn't feel okay." It was awkward, but it helped their friend own up and study harder next time. Jordan learned that integrity isn't about being perfect. It's about being brave enough to stand up for what's right.

"**Integrity** is doing the right thing, even when no one is watching." — C.S. Lewis

Personal Story: Textbook Temptation

In eighth grade, I forgot to bring my math textbook home the night before a big assignment was due. I panicked. My friend offered to give me all the answers. I stared at my book, thinking, *No one will know. Just copy and be done.*

But something didn't sit right. I hadn't even tried. It felt like cheating, because it was.

I ended up telling her: "Thanks, but I'm just going to turn it in late and explain to my teacher." I did. And honestly? She wasn't mad. She said, "Thanks for being honest. Let's come up with a plan so this doesn't happen again."

That moment taught me something big. Integrity isn't about being perfect, it's about being real. I still forget things sometimes, but I don't shortcut my values anymore. Every time I choose honesty, I feel a little stronger. And over time, people started to trust me more, not because I was flawless, but because I was honest.

Quick Quiz Box

Which of the following shows integrity?

A. Saying what people want to hear, even if it's not true
B. Blaming others to avoid consequences
C. Owning up to a mistake and making it right
D. Making excuses when you break a promise

(Answer: C)

Journal Reflection Box

When was a time you did the right thing, even though it was hard? How did it feel afterward?

Action Challenge Chart

Task	Goal	Outcome
Tell the truth, even when it's hard	Build honesty habit	Felt respected and lighter
Admit a mistake	Take responsibility	Gained trust from others
Keep a promise	Be reliable and consistent	Strengthened relationship

Mini-FAQ

Q1: What if being honest makes someone upset?
A: Integrity includes kindness. Be honest, but speak with care.

Q2: Do small lies really matter?
A: Yes. Small habits build big patterns. Integrity is built in the little things.

Q3: What if I mess up?
A: Integrity isn't about being perfect. It's about owning your mistakes and learning from them.

> **Leadership Ninja Takeaway**
>
> The world needs leaders who do the right thing, not just the easy thing. Choose integrity. It will always lead you somewhere good.

4

ORGANIZATION

The Secret to Organization

Organization is the foundation of leadership. It helps you manage your time, stay focused on your goals, and follow through on promises. A messy schedule leads to missed deadlines, forgotten responsibilities, and stress. But a Leadership Ninja? They're in control. They plan, prioritize, and prepare so that when opportunity knocks, they're ready to answer.

Here's why organization is a game-changer:

» It saves you time. When you know where things are and what needs to be done, you waste less time hunting for lost items or figuring out your next move.
» It lowers your stress. Clear plans and tidy spaces make your brain feel less overwhelmed. That means fewer meltdowns and more mental peace.
» It boosts your confidence. Staying on top of responsibilities makes you feel capable and proud of yourself.

- » It sets you apart. When teachers, coaches, and even friends see you're reliable and prepared, they trust you with leadership roles and opportunities.
- » It helps you reach your goals. Big dreams require small daily steps. Being organized helps you break down goals and actually achieve them.

Think of organization like a GPS for your life, it helps you get where you want to go faster and with less stress.

Why Do Leaders Need to Be Organized?

Being organized might not sound exciting, but it's actually one of the most powerful tools any leader can have.

When you've got a system, like checklists, planners, or digital reminders, you know what's coming and what you need to do. That means fewer late-night cram sessions, less stress, and way more peace of mind. You're not constantly reacting to chaos, you're staying ahead of it.

Organization also helps you set the vibe for everyone else. Leaders are the people others look to. If you're calm, collected, and on top of things, your team, classmates, or friends will trust you more. Being organized means you show up prepared, keep promises, and don't drop the ball, and that makes people feel safe following your lead.

Another benefit? You get more done in less time. When your stuff is together, you're not wasting time looking for a lost worksheet or trying to figure out what's due. You can focus, finish faster, and even have time to chill or do what you actually want to do.

It also gives your brain space for the big stuff. When you're not scrambling to remember everything, your mind is free to think creatively, start a new project, help a friend, solve a problem, or come up with a cool idea. Leaders need that mental space to plan ahead and dream big.

And finally, getting organized now is practice for real life. Whether you want to be a CEO, a teacher, an artist, or an athlete, every adult leader you admire has to stay on top of things. Learning how to be organized as a teen gives you a huge head start in whatever future you're building.

If Organization Is So Important… Why Is It So Hard?

Let's be real, if staying organized is such a game-changer, why aren't more teens doing it?

For starters, life gets busy *fast*. Between classes, homework, sports, clubs, group chats, family responsibilities, and trying to have a social life, it's a lot to keep track of. When things pile up, staying organized can feel like one more thing on your plate instead of the solution that makes life easier.

Another reason? No one really teaches it. You might hear adults say "be more organized," but what does that even mean? Most teens haven't been taught how to build routines, use planners effectively, or break big projects into smaller tasks. It's not about being lazy, it's about not knowing where to begin.

Also, your brain is still under construction. Seriously. The part of your brain that helps you plan, manage time, and stay focused (called the prefrontal cortex) is still developing during your teen years. So if organizing your life feels hard, that's because it is, but it's also a skill you can absolutely train.

And let's not forget: distractions are *everywhere*. With texts, social media, streaming, and endless apps grabbing your attention, it's easy to fall off track, even if you started organized. Your brain is in a constant battle for focus.

Lastly, organization takes effort, especially at first. Setting up systems, writing checklists, or planning out your week can feel annoying when you'd rather just chill. But here's the truth: a little effort up front saves a *lot* of chaos later. Once you experience the calm that comes from being in control of your time, it gets way easier to keep going.

The Sneaky Consequences of Disorganization

Disorganization isn't just about having a messy locker or a backpack full of crumpled papers. It goes deeper, and it's sneakier than you think.

When your stuff is all over the place, your brain starts to feel that way too. According to the American Psychological Association, physical clutter and a lack of structure can actually raise your cortisol levels (that's your body's stress hormone). This means your brain stays in "fight-or-flight" mode way longer than it needs to. Over time, this can make you feel anxious, tired, and mentally drained, even if you're not doing anything super stressful.

Disorganization can also steal your time. Ever spent 10 minutes looking for a homework sheet, your earbuds, or the right Zoom link? That time adds up. And when you're constantly scrambling, it's easy to miss deadlines, forget important dates, or feel like you're always behind. That "I'm drowning" feeling? It often starts with disorganization.

But here's the real leadership issue: disorganization affects how others see you. If you're always late, forgetting things, or barely holding it together, people may hesitate to rely on you, even if you're smart, kind, or talented. And worse, you might start doubting yourself too.

Leaders don't need to be perfect, but they do need to be dependable. When your space, schedule, and thoughts are in order, you create calm for both yourself *and* the people around you. You can respond instead of react. You can lead instead of scramble. You can breathe instead of panic.

The good news? Organization is a skill, not a personality trait. You're not "just messy", you might just need a system that works for you. Start small. One habit, one list, one shelf at a time. Because the more organized you feel, the more confident and capable you become.

Expert Advice

"When teens learn to organize their time and space, they gain confidence and reduce daily stress. Good organizational habits improve mental health, not just productivity."
— Dr. Sarah Jensen, Adolescent Psychologist

Actionable Strategies

The 3 C's
Get organized with this ninja life hack.

1. Collections: Create one place to collect everything, assignments, to-dos, reminders. Use a notebook, app, or folder.

2. Categories: Group similar tasks together. Ex: homework, chores, practice.

3. Checklists: Make small, checkable steps. Checking things off gives your brain a hit of dopamine, aka, a little win!

Relatable Teen Scenario

Amari used to forget everything, homework, practice times, even birthdays. Her backpack looked like a paper explosion, and she was always rushing or apologizing. One week, she forgot to turn in a big science project *and* missed soccer tryouts. That was the breaking point.

Her older cousin gave her a tip: "Write everything down, even the little stuff." Amari wasn't convinced, but she tried using a planner app and color-coded her classes. At first, it felt like extra work. But within a few weeks, she started feeling calmer. She stopped missing deadlines, had more time to chill, and even remembered her friend's birthday on time.

Now, Amari's the one reminding her friends when things are due. Her secret? It's not about being perfect, it's about having a plan that works *for her*.

"**For** every minute spent organizing, an hour is earned." — Benjamin Franklin

Personal Story: My First Organization Lesson

In 9th grade, I missed out on a field trip I had been looking forward to for weeks. It wasn't just any trip, we were going to a science museum with hands-on exhibits, and rumor had it there was a planetarium show and a make-your-own ice cream lab. I was so pumped... until I realized the night before that I had never turned in my permission slip.

I searched everywhere. Dug through my backpack. Checked under my bed. Nothing. I had totally spaced it, and my heart sank. I remember sitting in class that day while everyone else was loading onto the bus. My stomach twisted with regret. All I could think about was, *"Why didn't I just turn it in? How did I let this slip?"*

That moment hit me hard. It wasn't just about missing the museum, it was about missing opportunities. I realized that being unorganized didn't just make me late or stressed, it actually caused me to lose out on things I cared about.

After that, I decided to do something different. I downloaded a planner app on my phone and set weekly reminders. I started writing down homework, project due dates, even small stuff like "bring gym clothes" or "ask Mom for a ride." At first it felt weird, like I was being *too extra*. But within a few weeks, I noticed something: I was less stressed. I wasn't scrambling to finish things at the last minute. I felt in control. And when the next big trip came around, I was the first one with my permission slip turned in.

That field trip taught me more than where we were going. It taught me that *organization isn't about being perfect, it's about being prepared*. And sometimes, the cost of not being organized isn't just a grade or a deadline. It's an experience you can't get back.

Quick Quiz Box
ORGANIZATION

True or False

1. Organization only matters if you have a lot of responsibilities.
2. Being organized lowers stress.
3. Planners and lists are for perfectionists only.

(Answers: F, T, F)

Journal Reflection Box

What's one area of your life that feels disorganized? What could you do to make it better this week?

Action Challenge Chart

Task	Goal	Outcome
Create a "collection spot"	Keep all assignments in one place	Felt more in control
Make 1 checklist/day	Build routine & structure	Fewer forgotten tasks
Organize backpack weekly	Reduce chaos	Saved time finding materials

Mini-FAQ

Q1: What if I'm naturally messy?
A: Being organized is a skill, not a personality trait. You can learn it!

Q2: What's the fastest way to start?
A: Pick one system: a checklist, a calendar, or a clean space. Keep it simple.

Q3: Is it okay to forget sometimes?
A: Totally. The goal isn't perfection, it's progress.

Leadership Ninja Takeaway

Start small. One checklist today could lead to the confidence to lead tomorrow.

5

EFFORT

Why Effort Pays Off

Intelligence can open doors, but effort is what keeps you moving forward. Leadership Ninjas understand that grit, curiosity, and resilience matter more than IQ.

When teens focus too much on being "naturally smart," they avoid challenges that could help them grow. But when you focus on effort, you realize that your brain is like a muscle: the more you work it, the stronger it gets.

- » Effort builds momentum. Every time you try, you get a little better.
- » When you value effort, you take on challenges rather than avoid them.
- » Effort teaches patience and discipline, two key leadership skills.
- » People notice when you work hard, and they respect it.

Why Effort Matters So Much for Leaders

You don't have to be the smartest, most talented, or most experienced person in the room to be a great leader. But you *do* have to show up, and effort is how you show up every day.

Effort builds respect. People don't follow someone just because they have a title. They follow people who *do the work*. When others see you trying your best, asking questions, staying late to finish a task, or offering to help without being asked, they take notice. Your effort shows that you care, and that earns trust.

It also builds momentum. Leadership isn't about making giant leaps all at once, it's about taking small, consistent steps in the right direction. Even when you're tired, uncertain, or worried about failing, putting in effort keeps you moving. One small win leads to another, and before long, you're making serious progress.

Plus, effort helps you learn faster. You gain way more from *doing* than from just thinking or planning. Even when you make mistakes, your effort turns into experience, and experience sharpens both your confidence and your skills.

When you lead by example, your effort sets the tone. If you show up halfway and expect others to give their all, it doesn't work. But when you're fully committed, prepared, present, and putting in the work, it inspires everyone else to step up too.

And finally, effort shows you're committed. It tells the people around you, "*This matters to me. I'm not here to coast, I'm here to contribute.*" That's exactly the kind of energy real leaders bring to every challenge they face.

If Effort Is So Important… Why Don't More Teens Give It?

Let's be real, everyone *says* effort is important. But that doesn't mean it's easy. A lot of teens struggle with giving full effort, even when they care deep down. And there are actually some pretty understandable reasons why.

For starters, trying your best means putting your heart into something. And that can be scary. Some teens hold back on effort because they're afraid of failing. It feels safer to not try at all than to try and still fall short. But the truth is, effort is the only way we *learn* and grow. No one gets it right the first time. That's not failure, it's part of the process.

Another reason? We've all been tricked by social media highlight reels. It's easy to look at someone's "overnight success" and think things should come easy. So when something takes time, energy, and practice, it's tempting to give up or think, "Maybe I'm just not good at this." But behind every success is someone who kept showing up, even when no one was watching.

There's also the motivation myth. A lot of teens wait to feel inspired before putting in the work. But motivation isn't magic, it comes and goes. Real leaders don't wait to feel ready. They learn how to take action *anyway*, and effort becomes the spark that builds momentum.

And let's not forget one of the biggest blockers: exhaustion. Teens today are juggling so much, school, sports, friendships, family drama, social media. When you're drained, giving effort can feel impossible. That's why taking care of your body and mind is just as important as taking care of your goals.

Finally, effort takes time to pay off, and that can be frustrating. You don't always see results right away. But just like planting a seed, if you keep showing up, keep trying, and keep pushing, something will grow. Effort is never wasted, it just takes time to bloom.

The Sneaky Consequences of Valuing Intelligence Alone

We all love being called "smart." It feels good. But here's the problem: if you start believing that your value comes only from how smart you are, things can get tricky, fast.

When teens are praised only for their intelligence, it sends a silent message: "Being smart is who you are. Don't mess it up." That pressure can lead to fear, fear of trying new things, fear of failing, and fear of not living up to that "smart kid" label. Suddenly, instead of being curious or taking on challenges, you start avoiding anything that might make you look *less than perfect.*

This can lead to what psychologists call a fixed mindset, the belief that your intelligence is something you either have or don't.

And if you think your worth depends on being the smartest person in the room, you might avoid risks, procrastinate on hard tasks, or give up quickly when something doesn't come easily. You're not lazy, you're protecting your identity.

That's where the real danger lies: smart doesn't equal strong. Leaders don't grow by *looking* smart. They grow by *trying*, failing, and trying again. True confidence doesn't come from always knowing the answer, it comes from trusting yourself to figure things out, even when you don't.

So instead of clinging to being the "smart one," try being the effort one. The brave one. The curious one. Praise your hustle, not just your head. Because intelligence may open doors, but effort, resilience, and a willingness to learn are what carry you through them.

The Science Behind Effort Over Intelligence

For a long time, people believed that being smart was something you were either born with or not. But research has proven that's just not true. In fact, scientists now know that effort plays a bigger role in success than natural talent or intelligence, especially for teens.

Psychologist Dr. Carol Dweck from Stanford University discovered something powerful called the growth mindset. A growth mindset means believing that your brain can grow stronger through effort, challenges, and learning. Teens with a growth mindset are more likely to try new things, bounce back from failure, and succeed in the long run, even if they aren't the best right away. In one of her studies, students who were praised for how hard they worked (instead of how smart they were) actually chose harder problems and performed better over time.

And guess what? Science backs it up on a brain level too. Thanks to something called neuroplasticity, we know your brain isn't fixed, it changes and adapts based on how much you use it. Every time you try something challenging, your brain builds new pathways. The more you practice, the stronger those connections get. In other words, effort literally rewires your brain and helps you grow smarter.

You might've heard of the idea that it takes 10,000 hours of practice to become great at something. That's based on the work of researcher Anders Ericsson, who found that the best musicians, athletes, and performers weren't just naturally talented, they practiced more, with more focus and effort. Hard work beats talent almost every time.

Other scientists have found that when teens put in effort and see improvement, they feel more confident and motivated to keep going. This idea comes from something called Self-Determination Theory, which shows that feeling capable is what keeps people going, not being perfect, but making progress.

The takeaway? Effort is a superpower. It makes your brain stronger, builds confidence, and teaches you that success isn't about being the smartest kid in class, it's about showing up, trying again, and growing one step at a time.

Expert Advice

"Praising effort rather than intelligence builds resilience and confidence. It teaches teens to embrace challenges instead of avoiding them."
— Dr. Carol Dweck, Psychologist and Author of *Mindset*

Actionable Strategies

Effort Over Intelligence (E.O.I.)

1. Embrace Mistakes: They're not failures, they're part of learning.

2. Celebrate Effort: Reward yourself for showing up and trying, not just for getting it right.

3. Use Growth Language: Say, "I haven't figured it out yet," instead of "I can't do this."

Relatable Teen Scenarios

- Alex always got good grades without trying. But in high school, things got harder. Instead of asking for help, he gave up. He was afraid of not looking smart.
- Zoe used to struggle with math. She started going to tutoring and practicing daily. She didn't become a genius overnight, but she went from failing to a B+.

"**Success** is the sum of small efforts, repeated day in and day out." — Robert Collier

Personal Story: Effort Over Intelligence

When I was younger, I honestly believed that being "smart" meant you got things right the first time. It meant you didn't need help, didn't ask questions, and definitely didn't struggle. So when I started chemistry in high school and totally didn't get it, I panicked. The formulas made no sense. The labs confused me. And no matter how hard I stared at my textbook, it felt like my brain was frozen.

At first, I hid it. I thought, *"If I ask for help, people will think I'm not smart."* So I stayed quiet. But inside, I was overwhelmed and falling further behind each week. Eventually, I bombed a quiz, and it crushed me. That was my wake-up call.

I finally worked up the courage to ask for help. I signed up for tutoring, even though I felt embarrassed, and started studying every day after school. I made flashcards, asked a million questions, and practiced problems over and over. And little by little, something amazing happened. *I started to get it.* The more effort I put in, the more confident I felt. I went from feeling totally lost to actually enjoying chemistry. I even started helping my friends study!

That experience completely changed the way I saw intelligence. I realized being "smart" isn't about having all the answers, it's about having the *grit* to keep trying when things don't come easy. Effort helped me discover a strength I didn't even know I had. And now, I know that leaders aren't the ones who never mess up, they're the ones who don't quit when things get hard.

Quick Quiz Box

True or False

1. Being smart means you shouldn't need help.
2. Effort matters more than talent.
3. Mistakes are something to be ashamed of.

(Answers: F, T, F)

Journal Reflection Box

Write about a time you struggled with something. What helped you push through?

Action Challenge Chart

Task	Goal	Outcome
Try something hard	Practice persistence	Grew confidence
Ask for help	Learn through collaboration	Understood more, felt supported
Track your effort daily	Notice and celebrate consistency	Built strong learn

Mini-FAQ

Q1: What if I'm not naturally good at school?
A: That's okay! Success comes from effort, not just natural talent.

Q2: Is it embarrassing to ask for help?
A: No way. Asking for help shows strength, not weakness.

Q3: Can I really get smarter?
A: Yes! Your brain grows when you challenge it. That's called neuroplasticity.

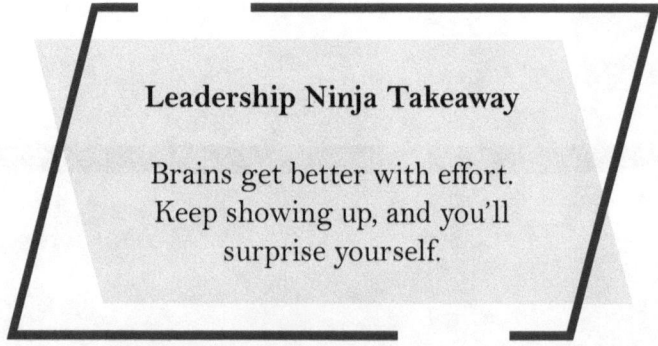

Leadership Ninja Takeaway

Brains get better with effort. Keep showing up, and you'll surprise yourself.

6

CALM

Why Calm?

Life can get loud, school, sports, social media, responsibilities. It's easy to feel overwhelmed, anxious, or just plain exhausted. That's why learning to stay calm is one of the most important skills a teen can develop.

Calm isn't the absence of chaos, it's the ability to manage your mind and body even when things get hectic. Calm leaders think before reacting. They bounce back from stress faster. And they help others feel more grounded, too.

Why Calm Is a Secret Weapon for Leaders

Being calm doesn't always get the spotlight in leadership books, but it should. Calm leaders don't just make people feel safe, they make better decisions, communicate more clearly, and create an environment where everyone can think, grow, and thrive.

When you're calm, you can respond instead of react. That's huge. Whether you're leading a group project, settling a disagreement, or stepping into a big moment like a presentation or competition, staying calm helps you *think before you act*. It keeps you from saying something you'll regret or making a snap decision based on emotions.

Calm is also contagious. Ever been around someone who totally loses it when things go wrong? It's stressful, right? Now think about someone who stays steady, even in the chaos. That energy spreads. Calm leaders help everyone else stay grounded, too. They bring a sense of "we've got this," even when things get tough.

Plus, staying calm protects your brain and your body. When you're constantly stressed or anxious, it's like running a marathon in your mind every day. It's exhausting, and it makes it harder to focus, remember things, or be creative. Calm doesn't mean you don't care. It means you care enough to take a breath and lead from a place of clarity.

Leaders face pressure all the time. The ones who rise above it are the ones who learn how to *reset*. Whether it's through deep breathing, a quick stretch, or a moment of stillness, calm is the anchor that lets you lead from your best self.

If Calm Is So Important… Why Is It So Hard?

Let's be honest, staying calm sounds great in theory. Who doesn't want to feel chill, centered, and in control? But for most teens (and adults too), calm isn't exactly the default setting. Life is loud, fast, unpredictable, and sometimes straight-up stressful.

One reason calm is hard is because stress is everywhere. School deadlines, friend drama, family expectations, social media pressure, it adds up. Your brain gets flooded with alerts and demands all day long, and before you know it, you're overwhelmed, annoyed, or about to snap. Calm doesn't feel like a priority when your mind is in panic mode.

Another reason? Most people aren't *taught* how to calm down. You might hear "just relax" or "don't overreact," but that's not helpful without tools. Learning how to breathe deeply, stretch out tension, or reset your nervous system takes practice, just like learning a sport or a new skill.

Plus, your brain is still developing, especially the part that handles impulse control and emotional regulation. That means it's completely normal to feel things more intensely as a teen. It's not about being dramatic, it's about your brain figuring out how to process and respond to big emotions. And that's hard when no one ever handed you a guidebook.

Also, a lot of teens confuse being calm with being passive. But calm isn't about ignoring your feelings or pretending everything's fine. It's about *pausing* before reacting. It's about knowing how to take a breath and make a better choice when you're upset, stressed, or overwhelmed.

The good news? Calm is a skill. It doesn't mean you're born peaceful, it means you've trained your body and mind to come back to center, no matter what's happening around you. And that skill? It makes you a stronger, wiser, and more powerful leader.

The Sneaky Consequences of Staying Stressed

Stress isn't always loud or obvious. Sometimes it creeps in quietly, tight shoulders, racing thoughts, snapping at someone without meaning to. At first, you might brush it off. "I'm just tired." "I've got a lot going on." But when stress builds without a release, it starts stacking up inside, like shaking a soda can over and over. Eventually, it bursts.

Constant stress affects more than just your mood, it impacts your entire system. Your sleep suffers, which means your brain doesn't get the chance to recharge. You might toss and turn all night, then struggle to focus the next day. Without enough rest, even small problems can start to feel huge.

Stress also messes with your immune system, making it easier to get sick. You might notice more headaches, stomach aches, or just feeling run-down all the time. It makes your body feel like it's always in "fight or flight" mode, even when there's no real danger.

Emotionally, staying stressed makes it harder to regulate your feelings. You might snap at someone over something small, cry more easily, or feel like you're carrying the weight of everything and can't explain why. Over time, this can lead to burnout, anxiety, or even depression.

For leaders, this is especially dangerous. When you're stressed out, it's harder to make good decisions, solve problems, or support others. You can't pour from an empty cup, and stress empties it fast.

That's why it's so important to build in reset moments. Whether it's deep breathing, stretching, walking outside, or talking it out, these small habits act like pressure valves. They let the steam out before things explode. Calm leaders lead better, not because they never feel stress, but because they've learned how to release it before it takes over.

What Stress Feels Like in the Body:

- » Tight shoulders or clenched jaw
- » Upset stomach or shallow breathing
- » Headaches or tired eyes
- » Feeling like you're "on edge" all day

Expert Advice

"Calm doesn't mean zoning out, it means being present and grounded. Mindful breathing and gentle movement help teens shift from fight-or-flight into rest-and-digest mode." — Dr. Lisa Damour, psychologist and author

Actionable Strategies

Deep Breathing + Ninja Yoga Flow

Step 1: **Deep Breathing**

- Inhale slowly through your nose for 4 seconds
- Hold for 4 seconds
- Exhale through your mouth for 6 seconds
- Repeat 3–5 times This calms your nervous system and helps reset your thoughts.

Step 2: **Ninja Yoga Flow.** Do this 5-minute flow to release tension, improve focus, and connect your body and mind.

1. Mountain Pose – Stand tall, reach arms up. Breathe deeply.
2. Downward Dog – Hinge at hips, hands and feet on the ground. Stretch and breathe.
3. Cat Pose – On hands and knees, round your back, chin to chest.
4. Cow Pose – Drop belly, lift head and tailbone. Inhale.
5. Boat Pose – Sit and lift legs off floor, engage core. Breathe slowly.
6. Seated Forward Fold – Sit, stretch hands toward feet. Relax into the stretch.

Relatable Teen Scenarios

- Skylar was stressed about finals. She did 5 rounds of deep breathing before her test, and felt her nerves fade away.
- Malik was about to lose it on his little brother. He paused, did the yoga flow, and came back ready to talk instead of yell.

"**Almost** everything will work again if you unplug it for a few minutes… including you." — Anne Lamott

Personal Story: My Experience with Yoga

I used to think taking breaks was a waste of time. I believed that if I wasn't constantly working, studying, or doing something "productive," I was being lazy. So I pushed myself hard. I filled my schedule with school, activities, projects, and responsibilities. On the outside, it looked like I had it all together. But inside, I was running on fumes.

The warning signs were there, I started getting headaches that wouldn't go away. I snapped at people I cared about. I had trouble sleeping. I couldn't focus. Everything felt *loud*. But I kept ignoring it because I thought rest meant weakness. I figured I just needed to "try harder."

One day, after a particularly stressful week, someone suggested I try yoga. I rolled my eyes. "Yoga? Isn't that just stretching and breathing?" But I was desperate, so I gave it a shot. I found a 10-minute video, cleared a tiny space in my room, and followed along.

And something weird happened.

As I moved through the poses, downward dog, mountain pose, cat-cow, and started breathing slowly, my mind started to quiet down. Not completely, but just enough for me to *notice* how tense I had been. That short session didn't fix all my problems, but it gave me something I hadn't felt in a long time: space. Space to breathe. Space to think. Space to feel.

That's when I realized calm isn't the opposite of productivity, it's what fuels it. When I started making time for short yoga flows or deep breathing during the day, I stopped burning out. I still had stress, but I wasn't ruled by it. I could think more clearly, respond more kindly, and lead with a level head.

Now, I know calm isn't a luxury, it's a leadership skill. And sometimes, the strongest thing you can do is *pause*.

Quick Quiz Box

True or False

1. Deep breathing only works for little kids.
2. Moving your body can help your brain calm down.
3. Being calm means ignoring your feelings.

Answers: (F, T, F)

Journal Reflection Box

When was the last time you felt totally calm? What helped you get there?

Action Challenge Chart

Task	Goal	Outcome
Try deep breathing daily	Reduce stress and anxiety	Felt lighter and more in control
Practice Ninja Yoga Flow	Relax muscles and calm the mind	Felt grounded and focused
Notice tension triggers	Build awareness around stress	Handled conflict more calmly

Mini-FAQ

Q1: What if I can't sit still?
A: That's okay! Start with movement-based calm like yoga or walking.

Q2: Does this really work in public or at school?
A: Yes. Even one slow breath in your seat can shift your state.

Q3: Is calm boring?
A: Nope. Calm is powerful. It's what helps you think clearly and act with purpose.

Leadership Ninja Takeaway

You don't have to control everything.
Just breathe, and return to calm.

PART II

IMPACTING OTHERS WITH YOUR LEADERSHIP

7

COLLABORATION

The Power of T.E.A.M.

Leadership isn't a solo sport. Even the most powerful leaders can't succeed without learning to work well with others. Collaboration is one of the most underrated leadership skills out there. Whether you're working on a school project, leading a sports team, or just trying to get through a group assignment, knowing how to collaborate can turn chaos into progress.

Collaboration means working together with others to reach a shared goal. It's about combining your strengths, listening to different perspectives, and supporting one another through challenges. In a true collaboration, everyone brings something valuable to the table, ideas, skills, effort, and decisions are made as a group, not just by one person.

For leaders, collaboration is essential. It shows that you trust your team, value others' input, and care more about the outcome than just being in charge. Collaboration doesn't mean everyone agrees all the time, it means you work through disagreements respectfully and find a solution together.

In short, collaboration turns "me" into "we", and that's where the real magic of leadership begins. When leaders know how to collaborate, they bring out the best in their team. They don't just bark orders or take over, they listen, encourage, and help everyone contribute. Great leaders know how to lead with others, not just over them.

Why Collaboration is So Hard For Some People

Collaboration can be hard for some people, especially teens, for a few reasons:

1. Fear of Losing Control
Some people are used to doing things their way. Letting others share the spotlight or influence the outcome can feel uncomfortable. When you're used to being in charge, or afraid things won't turn out "right", it's hard to trust others.

2. Past Group Project Trauma
Let's be real: not all group work is created equal. If someone's been stuck doing all the work while others slacked off, they might be hesitant to collaborate again. That past frustration can make teamwork feel more like a burden than a benefit.

3. Communication Struggles
Collaboration relies on clear, respectful communication, and not everyone feels confident speaking up or listening well. Misunderstandings, talking over each other, or avoiding hard conversations can derail teamwork fast.

4. Different Work Styles
Some people like to work ahead, others procrastinate. Some love big brainstorming sessions, while others prefer to think quietly first. When team members clash in how they work best, it takes patience and flexibility to meet in the middle.

5. Fear of Judgment

Sharing ideas can feel vulnerable. What if people don't like your idea? What if they think it's dumb? That fear can make people hold back, which stops true collaboration before it even starts.

The good news? Collaboration is a skill, and like all leadership skills, it can be learned, practiced, and improved with time. The key is showing up with an open mind, a willingness to listen, and the belief that you're better together.

Expert Advice

Dr. Tina Payne Bryson, co-author of *The Power of Showing Up*, says: "Feeling seen and supported helps teens take safe social risks, which is exactly what collaboration is."

When teens know their ideas matter, they're more likely to contribute. Leaders who encourage and validate others create teams where everyone feels safe to speak up. That psychological safety is the foundation of real collaboration, not just splitting tasks, but thinking together.

Actionable Strategies

T.E.A.M. Strategy

Here's a simple way to jumpstart collaboration. Remember T.E.A.M.:

- **T – Talk It Out**
  - » Good communication is the starting point for any successful team. Share your ideas, but also listen to what others are saying. Ask questions. Repeat what you hear to show you're listening. Respectfully disagree when needed. The more open and honest your conversations, the smoother your teamwork will be.
- **E – Encourage Everyone**
  - » The best teams don't just focus on the goal, they lift each other up. Cheer your teammates on. Notice their strengths. If

someone is struggling, offer help or kind words. Encouragement creates trust and brings positive energy to the group.
- **A – Agree on Roles**
  » Clear roles make things run better. Decide together who will do what. Who's leading the research? Who's designing the presentation? When everyone knows their role, it cuts down on confusion and makes people feel more responsible and valued.
- **M – Make Decisions Together**
  » Leadership means guiding, not controlling. Invite input from your team before making big decisions. Compromise when needed. The best solutions usually come from group input, not just one person's opinion. When people feel heard, they're more invested in the outcome.

You can use T.E.A.M. together, or just the one that hits hardest in the moment. They're flexible tools for any goal.

Relatable Teen Scenario

Sophia joined the drama club because she loves acting. But during rehearsals for the school play, things start falling apart. One kid keeps bossing everyone around, someone else always forgets their lines, and the set crew argues nonstop. Sophia feels frustrated, everyone's working *against* each other instead of *with* each other.

One day, instead of staying quiet, she speaks up:

"Hey guys, we all want this play to be great. What if we each take a part we're good at and check in every Friday?"

Surprisingly, people agree. The lead actor starts practicing lines with the shy cast members. The crew holds a mini brainstorm for set ideas. Rehearsals run smoother, and everyone starts to actually *have fun* again.

It wasn't magic, it was collaboration. All it took was one person willing to lead by listening and bringing everyone together.

"**Alone** we can do so little; together we can do so much." — Helen Keller

Personal Story: My Group Project Fiasco

In middle school, I had a group project where I ended up doing most of the work myself. I was annoyed, but I didn't really speak up or ask for help, I just assumed no one cared as much as I did. The result? I was stressed, my group was disconnected, and the final project was just okay.

Later, I realized the problem wasn't just the team, it was our lack of communication. I didn't use the T.E.A.M. strategy because I didn't know it yet. But once I learned to talk it out, encourage others, agree on roles, and make decisions together, everything changed. Future group projects became less stressful and way more fun, because I finally learned how to lead with my team, not just work around them.

Great leaders don't do it all alone. They collaborate, communicate, and create success together.

Quick Quiz Box

Which of the following is NOT part of the T.E.A.M. strategy?

A. Talk It Out
B. Eliminate Distractions
C. Agree on Roles
D. Make Decisions Together

(Answer: B)

Journal Reflection Box

Think about a recent group project, team activity, or club meeting.

- *What role did you naturally take?*
- *Did you feel heard and valued?*
- *Which part of the T.E.A.M. strategy do you want to practice more next time?*

COLLABORATION

Action Challenge Chart

Group Task	Talk It Out	Encourage Everyone	Agree on Roles	Make Decisions Together
Science Project	Ask for ideas before planning	Complimented a teammate's idea	Divided the slideshow tasks	Voted on design as a team
Fundraiser Club	Suggested a new idea	Cheered someone who was nervous	Volunteered for poster making	Decided goals together
Group Chores	Said, "Let's plan together!"	Said "Thanks for helping!"	Took out trash, others swept	Agreed on finish time

Mini-FAQ

Q1: What if someone in my group is super controlling?
A: Try "Talk It Out" from the T.E.A.M. strategy. Say something like, "I want to help too, can we make sure everyone has a role?"

Q2: What if nobody's doing anything and I'm stuck with all the work?
A: Ask to "Agree on Roles" out loud. Say, "Let's divide this so it's fair and we all get it done faster."

Leadership Ninja Takeaway

True leaders know that it's not about
doing everything themselves, it's
about helping others bring their best too.
That's what makes teams powerful.

8

GRATITUDE

The Magic of Appreciation

Gratitude isn't just about saying thank you, it's about noticing the good in your life, even when things aren't perfect. Practicing gratitude has been proven to improve mental health, boost happiness, and make relationships stronger. When teens focus on what they appreciate, they become more grounded, positive, and connected to others.

Grateful leaders inspire loyalty, kindness, and trust. Why? Because when you appreciate others, you make them feel seen and valued. Gratitude also helps you stay resilient during tough times by shifting your mindset from "What's wrong?" to "What's still right?"

Why Gratitude Is a Secret Leadership Superpower

A lot of people think leadership is all about giving orders, being in charge, or having the right answers. But real leaders, *great* leaders, know that leadership is about people. And that's where gratitude comes in.

Gratitude helps you see the good in others and makes them feel valued. When you're leading a team, club, class project, or even just your group of friends, showing appreciation builds trust. It helps people feel seen. And people who feel seen are way more likely to show up, speak up, and give their best.

Being grateful also shifts your mindset. Instead of focusing on what's going wrong or what's missing, it helps you pay attention to what *is* going right. That mindset doesn't just make you more optimistic, it makes you *resilient*. Because when you can find something to be grateful for, even during hard times, it becomes easier to stay calm, grounded, and motivated.

Gratitude is also contagious. When you thank someone, write a kind note, or just say "I appreciate you," it lifts everyone's mood, including your own. Leaders who lead with gratitude inspire others to do the same, creating teams, classrooms, and communities that are more positive, supportive, and strong.

So while gratitude might seem like a small thing, it's actually a *huge deal*. It helps you connect with others, bounce back from challenges, and create a vibe that people want to be part of. That's what real leadership is all about.

If Gratitude Is So Powerful… Why Don't More Teens Practice It?

Gratitude sounds simple, right? Say "thank you," appreciate what you have, and focus on the good. So if it's so important, why don't more teens do it regularly?

For starters, life moves fast. Between school, sports, group chats, social media, and everything else, it's easy to be on autopilot. When you're rushing from one thing to the next, you don't always pause to appreciate the little things, like a friend who texts to check in, or a teacher who gives you a second chance on an assignment.

Also, we live in a world that constantly tells us we need more. More likes, more clothes, more accomplishments. That kind of pressure makes it harder to notice what you already have going for you. Gratitude gets pushed to the side because the focus is on what's missing instead of what's meaningful.

Some teens also think that showing appreciation makes them look soft, awkward, or even cheesy. But the truth is, gratitude is actually a sign of strength. It takes confidence to thank someone, to compliment a friend, or to recognize your own growth. It's way easier to scroll past the good stuff than to stop and say, "Hey, that really mattered to me."

And then there's the simple fact that we're all human. Some days are tough. When you're feeling stressed, annoyed, or overwhelmed, gratitude might be the *last* thing on your mind. But those are actually the moments when it can help the most. It's like a flashlight in the dark, it doesn't make everything perfect, but it helps you see what's still shining.

Gratitude isn't just about being polite. It's about being aware, present, and connected. And while it might take a little effort at first, once you start practicing it, you'll see how powerful it really is.

The Sneaky Consequences of Taking Things for Granted

When you're constantly thinking about what you *don't* have, like the newest phone, better grades, or more followers, it's easy to fall into what's called the *comparison trap*. That's when you start measuring your worth by someone else's highlight reel. Suddenly, your A- doesn't feel good enough because your friend got an A+. Your sneakers feel old because someone else just got the newest drop. Your life starts to look "less than", even when it's actually full of amazing stuff.

Taking things for granted makes it hard to see your own progress. You forget how far you've come or how much support you actually have. You start chasing more, more, more… and it never feels like enough. That mindset doesn't just hurt your happiness, it drains your motivation. After all, why try your best if it's never going to feel like it matters?

For leaders, this is a big deal. If you're focused only on what's missing, it's hard to celebrate your team's wins or appreciate the people helping you along the way. You might start to expect things from others instead of appreciating them. That kind of attitude can lead to burnout, broken trust, and missed opportunities for connection.

On the flip side, practicing gratitude changes everything. When you start noticing what's going *right*, your brain literally rewires to focus on the positive. You feel more motivated, more connected, and more confident. You start to see that small things, like a kind text, a sunny day, or a good night's sleep, actually *are* big things.

Gratitude isn't just about saying "thanks." It's about training your brain to see the good that's already around you, so you can lead from a place of abundance, not emptiness.

Expert Advice

"Gratitude is one of the most powerful tools for emotional well-being. Teens who practice gratitude report fewer symptoms of depression, better sleep, and stronger relationships." — Dr. Robert Emmons, gratitude researcher and author

Actionable Strategies

The 5 Gs
Grow your gratitude with this ninja life hack.

1. **G**row our thank-yous and pleases.

2. **G**ift ourselves a gratitude jar.

3. **G**ive gratitude at the dinner table and before bedtime.

4. **G**et a gratitude journal.

5. **G**o on a gratitude nature walk.

Relatable Teen Scenarios

- Ty was always complaining about practice until he got injured. Sitting out made him realize how much he missed being part of the team.
- Jess wrote thank-you notes to her teachers during finals week. She thought it was cheesy, but they were so touched, and it made her feel more connected and appreciated too.

"**Gratitude** turns what we have into enough."
— Melody Beattie

Personal Story: The Tiny Thing That Changed Everything

There was a year I had to move schools right in the middle of the school year. It wasn't planned, and I definitely wasn't excited about it. I was leaving behind my friends, my routines, and everything familiar. On my first day at the new school, I felt completely out of place. I didn't know where anything was, didn't recognize a single face, and honestly just wanted to disappear.

I remember sitting alone in the cafeteria, staring at my lunch, pretending to be busy on my phone. That's when a girl walked up to me and asked, "Hey, want to sit with us?" It seemed like such a small thing at the time, but to me, it meant *everything*. She didn't have to include me. She didn't have to notice I was alone. But she did.

She introduced me to her friends and even gave me a quick tour of the school. That one simple act of kindness changed my entire experience. I started making friends, I got more involved, and slowly, I started to feel like I belonged again. Her gesture wasn't loud or dramatic, it was quiet, kind, and full of heart. And it stuck with me.

From that day forward, I promised myself I would never underestimate the power of a small, kind action. Now, I try to *look* for the good, whether it's someone helping out, including others, or just showing up with a smile. I also make it a point to say thank you, out loud. Because gratitude isn't just something you feel, it's something you *share*. And those moments, as tiny as they seem, have the power to completely change someone's day, or even their life.

Quick Quiz Box

True or False

1. Gratitude is just about being polite.
2. You can be grateful even when life is hard.
3. Saying thank you doesn't make a difference.

(Answers: F, T, F)

Journal Reflection Box

Who is one person you're grateful for right now? What would you say to them?

Action Challenge Chart

Task	Goal	Outcome
Write 3 things you're grateful for	Build a daily gratitude habit	Felt calmer and more positive
Send a thank-you text	Strengthen connection with someone	Made their day—and yours
Say thanks before eating	Practice presence and appreciation	Ate more mindfully

Mini-FAQ

Q1: What if I don't feel grateful?
A: That's normal. Gratitude isn't about ignoring problems, it's about seeing what's still good.

Q2: Can gratitude really improve my mood?
A: Yes! Studies show it can lower stress, boost optimism, and even help with sleep.

Q3: Do I have to write it down?
A: Writing helps your brain remember and focus, but even thinking grateful thoughts works.

Leadership Ninja Takeaway

Gratitude is fuel for your heart.
The more you notice the good,
the more good you'll find.

9

COMMUNICATION

Communication is the glue that holds relationships, teams, and leadership together. Whether you're giving a presentation, talking with a teacher, or resolving a disagreement with a friend, the way you express yourself can either build bridges or create walls. Great leaders aren't just good at talking, they're great at connecting.

Clear communication builds trust. It prevents misunderstandings, keeps teams on the same page, and helps people feel seen and heard. And when you know how to communicate with kindness and confidence, people are more likely to listen, support your ideas, and follow your lead.

Why Communication Is a Leadership Superpower

Being a great leader isn't about having all the answers, it's about making sure everyone understands the mission, feels heard, and knows where they're going. That's where communication comes in.

When leaders communicate clearly, they set the tone for everything else. They help teams avoid confusion, solve problems faster, and build trust. Whether you're giving directions, sharing ideas, or just checking in on a friend, the way you say things matters.

Words can motivate, connect, and calm. Or they can confuse, divide, and hurt. Leaders choose their words with care.

But communication isn't just about talking. Great leaders are also great listeners. They know that paying attention to others shows respect, helps them learn, and builds stronger relationships. Listening tells people, *You matter*. And when people feel valued, they're more likely to work together, speak up, and follow your lead.

Good communication is like a bridge. It connects ideas, people, and emotions, and strong leaders build those bridges every day.

If Communication Is So Important… Why Is It So Hard?

Let's be real, if communication is such a leadership superpower, why aren't more teens amazing at it?

For starters, most people aren't *taught* how to communicate well. You might hear "use your words," but no one really breaks down *how*. Things like active listening, choosing kind words, or expressing your feelings without blaming others aren't always part of school or home life.

Then there's technology. We're texting, snapping, and DMing more than talking face-to-face. That means we miss out on tone, facial expressions, and body language, all the stuff that helps us really *get* each other. It's easy to misread a message or come off harsh without meaning to.

Also, emotions can get in the way. When you're stressed, angry, or anxious, it's way harder to say things calmly or clearly. Instead of pausing to think, you might blurt something out, or say nothing at all.

And let's not forget fear. Many teens stay quiet because they're afraid of being misunderstood, sounding awkward, or getting judged. Speaking up takes courage, and it's something you build with practice, not something you're born with.

The good news? Communication *can* be learned. With tools like the C.L.U.E. strategy, practice, and a little self-awareness, you can go from awkward to awesome, and become the kind of leader others want to listen to and follow.

The Sneaky Consequences of Poor Communication

When communication breaks down, everything else tends to follow. You might have the best ideas, the kindest heart, or the strongest work ethic, but if you can't express yourself clearly, those strengths can get lost in translation.

Poor communication creates confusion. People misunderstand instructions, make assumptions, or get stuck waiting for clarification. What started as a small task turns into a big mess because no one was sure what to do or how to do it.

It also leads to conflict. When you don't explain your thoughts, needs, or feelings in a respectful way, others may take it the wrong way. A misunderstood tone in a text, a sarcastic joke that lands wrong, or a silent treatment when you're upset, all of these can build tension fast. Friends can grow distant. Group projects can fall apart. Teams can become divided. And worst of all, the damage often lingers longer than the original problem.

Missed deadlines and dropped responsibilities are common side effects too. If expectations aren't communicated clearly, things slip through the cracks. Everyone ends up frustrated, and trust starts to break down.

And then there's the emotional toll. Poor communication can make you feel invisible, unheard, or unimportant. You might feel like no one listens to you, or that your ideas don't matter. That's not just frustrating, it can be incredibly discouraging, especially for a young leader trying to find their voice.

What does it feel like in real life?

Awkward group chats. Misunderstood tone in texts. People rolling their eyes or ignoring your suggestions. Feeling like you're always explaining yourself, or never being given the chance to.

It can make you feel tense, left out, or unsure of yourself.

The good news? Communication isn't a personality trait, it's a skill. And like any skill, it gets better with practice. Whether you're leading a team, navigating friendships, or advocating for yourself, better communication helps you build stronger connections, avoid unnecessary drama, and lead with clarity and confidence.

Expert Advice

Dr. Brené Brown, researcher and author, says, "Clear is kind. Unclear is unkind." Being direct with compassion is one of the best tools a leader can develop. You don't need fancy words or a loud voice, just honesty, empathy, and a willingness to listen.

Actionable Strategies

Use the C.L.U.E.

There's an easy way to improve communication. Just remember the C.L.U.E.

- » **C**hoose positive words over negative ones.
- » **L**isten, really listen, without interrupting.
- » **U**se "I" instead of "you" to express your feelings.
- » **E**nd with a thank you.

You don't have to use all of them every time, but any of these tools can make a conversation better.

Relatable Teen Scenario

Jordan was leading a school project, and the group wasn't listening to her ideas. She snapped and said, "You never care what I think!" The room went silent. Later, she tried again: "I feel frustrated when I don't feel heard. Can we all take turns next time?" It made a huge difference. The group started working better together, and Jordan learned that how you speak changes what people hear.

"**The** single biggest problem in communication is the illusion that it has taken place." – George Bernard Shaw

Personal Story: My First Argument as a Leader

During my first student council meeting, I was so excited to share an idea I had been working on for days. I thought everyone would love it. But one of the other members immediately disagreed. They said it wouldn't work and offered a different approach. I froze, then snapped. "You just don't get it!" I blurted, way louder than I meant to.

Instantly, the mood in the room shifted. People went quiet. I could see the tension I had caused. In that moment, I felt embarrassed, frustrated, and misunderstood all at once. But later, I sat with what had happened and realized the problem wasn't their disagreement, it was how I reacted.

I hadn't listened. I was so focused on being right that I didn't hear what they were actually saying. I also used blaming words, "you", instead of owning how I felt. That night, I replayed the meeting in my head and practiced how I could've responded better.

At the next meeting, I took a breath and said, "I felt discouraged when my idea was dismissed, and I really want to understand your perspective better." I could feel the room soften. People made eye contact again. We had a real conversation. And to my surprise, our two ideas actually combined into something even stronger.

That moment didn't just teach me how to lead a project. It taught me how to lead people, with humility, curiosity, and clear communication. I didn't earn their respect because I had the best idea. I earned it because I showed I was willing to learn, listen, and grow. And that's what real leadership looks like.

Quick Quiz Box

Which of the following is the most effective way to express frustration?

A. "You never help!"
B. "I feel stressed when I have to do this alone."
C. "Whatever."

(Answer: B)

Journal Reflection Box

Think of a time when you didn't feel heard. How did you respond? How could you use the C.L.U.E. method if it happened again?

Action Challenge Chart

Day	Who You Talked To	CLUE Step You Used	What Happened?
Mon	Sister	Listen	Less arguing
Tue	Teacher	Use "I" statement	Clearer convo
Wed	Friend	Positive words	Smiles returned

Mini FAQ

Q1: What if I get nervous talking out loud?
A: Start small. Practice with friends or write out what you want to say. Confidence comes with practice.

Q2: How do I listen better?
A: Focus on what the other person is saying instead of what you'll say next. Nod, ask questions, and repeat back to show you understand.

> ### Leadership Ninja Takeaway
>
> Communication is a leadership superpower. Use your C.L.U.E. to build trust, express yourself clearly, and lead with confidence.

COMMUNICATION

FINAL THOUGHTS

YOUR JOURNEY TO LEADERSHIP

Leadership isn't just about standing at the front of the room or being the loudest voice. True leadership starts with you, your choices, your habits, and how you treat yourself and others. Throughout this book, you've explored what it means to be Organization, Effort, Gratitude, Calm, Focus, Courage, Integrity, Communication, and Collaboration. ☺

Each Ninja skill is like a tool in your backpack. The more tools you collect, the more confident and prepared you'll feel. Some days will feel easy. Others, not so much. But that's okay, leadership is a journey, not a destination.

When you prioritize your mindset, your health, your relationships, and your goals, you grow into someone others want to follow. Someone who lifts others up. Someone who leads by example.

So here's your final challenge: Keep showing up. Keep growing. Keep leading like a Ninja.

You've got this!

NINJA MOVES GLOSSARY

B.R.A.V.E. Strategy – A method to build courage: Breathe, Relax your muscles, Adopt positive body language, Visualize success, Embrace a mantra.

Calm Ninja Flow – A yoga-inspired series of poses to help reset your mind and body: Downward Dog, Mountain Pose, Cow Pose, Cat Pose, and Boat Pose.

F.O.C.U.S. Method – A strategy to improve concentration: Find distractions and eliminate them, Organize, Choose leafy vegetables and healthy foods, Use exercise, Split up large tasks.

Gratitude Practice – The daily habit of noticing and appreciating the good things in life.

Mindful Breathing – A calm and controlled breathing technique that helps reset your nervous system.

The 3 C's – A method to keep your life in order using Categories, Collections, and Checklists.

T.E.A.M.– A strategy for collaboration. Talk it out, encourage everyone, agree on roles, make decisions together

S.T.R.E.T.C.H. – Not in this book, but you've probably been doing it anyway

You did it, Ninja! Now go lead the way.

LEADERSHIP NINJA CHALLENGES (ACTIVITIES TO BUILD LEADERSHIP SKILLS)

These fun, practical challenges are designed to help you flex your leadership muscles every day. Complete them at your own pace and repeat your favorites!

1. The Morning Mastery Challenge
Wake up 30 minutes earlier for 3 days to practice mindfulness, organize your day, and eat a healthy breakfast.

2. One Brave Thing a Day
Do something outside your comfort zone daily for a week, raise your hand in class, apologize first, or try something new.

3. The Gratitude Shoutout
Each day, message or tell one person something you appreciate about them. Notice how it strengthens your relationships.

4. Collaboration Tracker
Use T.E.A.M. to help you collaborate with others. Pick one project and evaluate how you work with others.

5. Communication C.L.U.E.
The next time you have a conversation with someone check to see how much you listen and use the C.L.U.E.

6. F.O.C.U.S. Mission
Pick one school assignment and apply the F.O.C.U.S. method. Break it into steps, clear distractions, and set a timer.

7. Calm Ninja Flow Break
When you're overwhelmed, do the Calm Ninja Flow (Downward Dog, Mountain, Cat/Cow, Boat Pose). Repeat 3x.

8. The Organizer Overhaul
Choose one area, your room, backpack, or phone, and use the Categories, Checklists + Checklists method to declutter.

9. Leadership Reflection Journal
Write about a time you made a good decision. What did you learn? What would you do differently?

Bonus Challenge: Lead a Leadership Ninja Club Start a club at school or online where you share Ninja skills, do challenges together, and lift each other up. Being a leader starts with lifting others!

Remember: Consistency beats perfection. Keep practicing, and leadership will become part of who you are.

Other Products by Mary Nhin

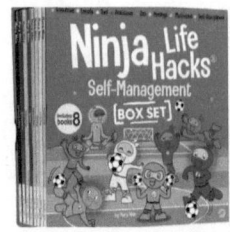

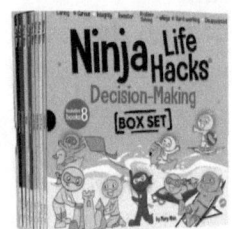

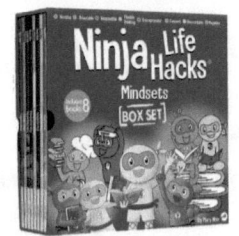

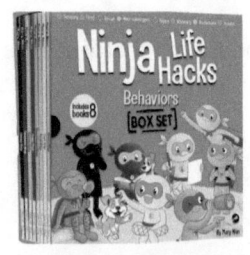

NinjaLifeHacks.tv

About the Author

Mary Nhin is a social impact entrepreneur and author of the flagship series, Ninja Life Hacks, a social-emotional learning brand, with 124 books and 99 characters, dedicated to empowering children with life skills. It's captured the hearts of over four million readers and continues to lead the way for an exciting adventure in social, emotional learning.

At the core of Mary Nhin's writing is a flicker of hope. While the writer frequently lays her soul bare, tackling issues such as failures, acceptance, and loneliness, there's always a silver lining. That's particularly true of her book series, "Ninja Life Hacks," which looks at failures as a transformative experience.

Under Mary's leadership, the Ninja Life Hacks brand of books, resources, and toys have empowered people worldwide with social, emotional coping strategies to use for a lifetime. Her books have been translated in twelve countries.

As Co-founder and Chief Creative Officer of Nhinja Sushi, the mom and pop restaurant has blossomed into a five location restaurant chain, serving up high quality sushi and freshly cooked meals to busy families. Today, over 1500+ people visit Nhinja locations daily.

Mary's visionary leadership earned her and her teams a collection of industry accolades including: Woman of Integrity Award Winner (Better Business Bureau), Most Admired CEO (The Journal Record), HER award (405 Magazine), Top 50 Most Influential Oklahomans Power List (Journal Record), Top 100

Small Businesses (U.S. Chamber of Commerce), AAPI Strong Restaurant Winner (National ACE), In the Lead Female Leader (Journal Record), 40 Under Forty (OKC Business), Inc 5000 (Inc. Magazine), Best Sushi (Edmond Life and Leisure and Edmond Sun), Best Finance Books For Kids (Investopedia), Best Kids Money Books (Mom.com).

    She and her husband, Kang Nhin, are proud parents of three children, Mikey, Kobe, and Jojo.

WEBSITE: www.ninjalifehacks.tv

WEBSITE: www.nhinja.com

LINKEDIN: @Marynhin

FB: Nhinja Sushi

FB: Ninja Life Hacks

IG: @nhinjasushi

IG: @officialninjalifehacks

TT: @officialninjalifehacks

YT: youtube.com/@NinjaLifeHacks

X: @nhinjas

Email: mary@ninjalifehacks.tv

www.ingramcontent.com/pod-product-compliance
Lightning Source LLC
LaVergne TN
LVHW041614070526
838199LV00052B/3141